CW00666677

THE WISDOM OF ST TERESA OF AVILA

THE
WISDOM
OF
ST TERESA
OF AVILA

Compiled and introduced by
Ruth Burrows

LION
Giftlines

This edition copyright © 1998 Lion Publishing

Published by
Lion Publishing plc
Sandy Lane West, Oxford, England
ISBN 0 7459 3976 7

First edition 1998
10 9 8 7 6 5 4 3 2 1 0

A catalogue record for this book is available
from the British Library

Printed and bound in Singapore

Designer: Philippa Jenkins

CONTENTS

INTRODUCTION

St Teresa of Avila was born in 1515 and died in 1582. A legend in her native Spain during the last twenty years of her life, the magic of her personality pervades her writings with its captivating power. But more important is the fascination evoked by the sense that here we meet a human person not merely in living contact with God as are many others, but vividly aware of this contact, this immersion in divine waters, and able in some sort to look at and analyse the relation of the human person to the Divine Creator. The Church has given solemn recognition to Teresa's 'authority' in speaking of things divine with the title 'Doctor of Mystical Theology'.

Yet we can easily be misled. This bewitching woman was richly endowed with a wide range of gifts: an astute head for business and organization; considerable literary talent; a genius for friendship that, in her earlier years, led her astray; amazing courage and strength, heartening, supporting others even though in need of reassurance and love herself; tender, 'hard' as occasion demanded – these are but a selection. Nevertheless, like the rest of us, she had her weaknesses and was conditioned by the times in which she lived. Indeed, it could be said that a woman of such sensitivity and impressionability, thirsting for experience of life, would be more than ordinarily influenced by the climate of her age and country. So it is. A well-known feature of Teresa's life and writings is the plethora of 'spiritual experiences'. Is it this, precisely, that has won for her the title, Doctor of Mystical Theology? Surely not, and yet often enough it is this feature which dazzles us and we overlook what she herself reiterates time and time again: that, in themselves, spiritual 'favours', no matter how sublime they seem, give no certainty of holiness and it is dangerous to desire them. Moreover, our modern insight into the mystery of the human psyche – an insight always limited, ever open to surprises – especially of the dimension that we call the unconscious, applauds this objective appraisal of Teresa. It must be acknowledged, however, that she herself was enamoured of 'favours' and was too dependent on them, conscious that they had, so she believed, brought her immense benefits. We should not shrink from admitting that this was a weakness on her part. A theologian who knew her well, who loved and respected her, perceiving the danger, expressed the desire to see her safely dead! It is probably true to say that Teresa attained great holiness not through them but in spite of them. Her humility and passion for God immunized her from harmful consequences. God is utterly faithful; as she herself declares, if we try with all our heart to please Him, He will turn heaven and earth upside down rather than let us come to harm.

We honour Teresa and glorify her God by seeing her in truth and recognizing where lay her true greatness: her passion for God's will and her incredible generosity of response; the slightest awareness that God asked anything of her and she was up and about, a sick, elderly woman, accomplishing the impossible, enduring hardships of every kind and not least slander and persecution.

'Oh, how dear He is!' and for this dear One she gave her all without hesitation or stint. The intimacy, the union with Christ her Lord, her dear One, which illumines every page of her writings, was not derived from nor nourished principally by her visions. We should see these phenomena in a general way as 'images' that her mind, her psyche used to express in some way what really mattered, the union of her surrendered self with God. All that made Teresa a great mystic, a passionate lover of God, is available to each of us if we would take the same path of faithful prayer, humble perseverance and generosity in doing God's will and not our own, and a tireless effort to love others as Jesus has loved us. The Teresa of visions and ecstasies remains on the pedestal, out of reach; an object of delight and admiration but unchallenging. The real Teresa speaks directly to us: true union can be attained, 'with our Lord's help, if we really try for it by surrendering our own will to whatever is the will of God… Oh how much to be desired is this union! Happy the soul that has attained it!' and again, 'Beg our Lord to give you perfect love for your neighbour and leave the rest to Him.'

RUTH BURROWS

GOD WITH US

I

RICHES WITHIN

We so rarely reflect on the riches within our souls, who dwells there, or how precious they are, and so do little to preserve their beauty.

Interior Castle M:1 c:1

2

THE DIVINE IMAGE

I was recollected in the divine companionship
which I have always in my soul, and it seemed
to me that God was present therein in such a
way that I recalled St Peter's words: 'You are
Christ, the Son of the living God', for the
living God was in my soul. This is not like
other visions, for it overpowers faith; so that it
is impossible to doubt that the Trinity dwells
in our souls by presence, power and essence.
To know this truth is the very highest gain;
and as I stood wondering to see His Majesty
in a thing so vile as my soul, I heard: 'It is not
vile, my child, for it is made in my image.'

Relation 9

DELIGHT IN GOD

When I remember how You say that You
find Your delights with Your human children,
I am filled with joy… When Your Son was
baptized, Your voice was heard declaring that
You delighted in Him. Is it really true that You
delight in us as in Him? Rejoice, my heart,
that there is One Who loves your God as He
deserves. Rejoice that there is One Who fully
knows His goodness and how great He is.
Thank Him, my heart, for having given to our
earth One Who really knows Him – His only
Son. With His protection you can approach
His Majesty and entreat Him, that, since He
delights in you, He will ensure that nothing
on earth will deter you from finding all your
delight in Him.

Exclamations 7

THE INTERIOR CASTLE

Let us imagine our soul as a castle, one made
out of a single diamond or translucent crystal,
and that there are many rooms in this castle…
Think carefully over this and realize that the
soul of a good person is nothing less than a
paradise, in which, as God tells us Himself,
He finds delight. Imagine how beautiful that
dwelling must be to delight a King so mighty,
so wise, so pure and abounding in goodness.
I can find nothing whatever to compare in
beauty with the human soul in its vast capacity.
No matter how powerful our intellect may be,
we can no more comprehend this than we can
comprehend God Himself; for according to
His own word, He made us in His image and
likeness…

The human soul is a creature, of course,
and there is therefore as much difference
between it and God as between creature and
Creator, but the fact that His Majesty says it
is made in His own image means that we can

hardly form any idea of its great dignity and
beauty… This castle, as I have said, is made
up of many rooms; some above, some below
and others at either side; and in the midst of
them is that chamber which is the inmost
heart of the castle where secret intimacies are
exchanged between God and the soul.

Interior Castle M:1 c:1

THE TREE OF LIFE

I want you to consider what the castle of our
soul would be like, so beautiful, shining in
splendour, this Orient pearl, this tree of life,
planted in the life-giving waters — namely, in
God — were we to commit grievous sin. There
is no darker darkness. But the point I want
to make is that, although the Sun Himself,
Who gives it all its beauty and splendour,
is still there in its centre… the soul cannot
participate in Him no more than can a crystal,
covered with a dark cloth, reflect the sun's
light… Just as all the streams that flow from
a clear spring are as pure as the spring itself,
so the works that flow from a soul in a state
of grace are beautiful in the eyes of God, and
beautiful in human eyes also, for they come
from the stream of life in which the tree of
the soul is planted.

Interior Castle M:1 c:2

DIVINE FRIENDSHIP

As you are alone, look for a companion and
where will you find a better Companion than
the Master who teaches you the Our Father,
the prayer you are about to say? Think of this
Lord as at your side, teaching you so lovingly
and humbly. Believe me, you should stay with
a Friend like this for as long as you possibly
can. If you form the habit of remembering
that He is always at your side, and He sees
that you love His companionship and are
always intent on pleasing Him, it will become
impossible for you ever to send Him away and
He will never let you down. He will be there,
helping you to bear your trials and you will
find Him everywhere. Do you consider it a
small thing to have such a Friend as this at
your side?

Way of Perfection c.26

INTERIOR PRAYER

THE GATEWAY TO GOD

As far as I can understand, the gateway to
this castle is prayer and meditation. I am
not referring only to mental prayer, for vocal
prayer if genuine is necessarily meditative. If
we do not reflect on Whom we are addressing
and what we are asking for and what we are
who are doing the asking and the nature of the
One whom we ask then I cannot think we are
praying at all even though our lips are busy
mouthing prayers. It is true that sometimes
we can pray without specifically averting to
these things but that is because they have been
carefully considered beforehand. But merely to
utter words that we know by heart and that
readily spring to the lips, that is not prayer —
and God grant that none of us Christians ever
speaks to God like that!

Interior Castle M:1 c:1

OUR CLOSEST COMPANION

Turn your eyes upon yourself and look deep
within. There you will find your Master…
I should like to find words to explain what it
is, this holy companionship with the Companion
of our souls, the Holiest of holies, wherein is
no obstacle to hinder the soul and her Spouse
from remaining alone together any time the soul
chooses to enter within herself and shut the door
behind her, so as to keep out everything worldly
and to dwell in that Paradise with her God. I say
'chooses' because you must understand that I am
not referring to a supernatural state but one that
depends on our choice and that, by God's grace,
we can enter of our own accord… All I want is
that we should recognize and stay with the
Person with whom we are speaking… The
trouble is that we do not really grasp the fact that
He is near us and imagine Him far away – so far,
that we should have to go to Heaven in order to
find Him. Why, O Lord, do we not look at Your
face, when it is so near us?

Way of Perfection c:29

THE DIVINE PRESENCE

Remember how St Augustine tells us that, after seeking God everywhere, he found Him within himself. It is no small matter for those of us who are often distracted to grasp this truth and to find that, if we want to speak to our Eternal Father and to enjoy His presence, we don't have to go to heaven or to speak in a loud voice. The softest whisper is heard. He is so near: we need no wings to fly in search of Him but have only to be alone and look upon Him present within us... We must talk to Him very humbly, ask Him for what we need as we would ask a father, tell Him our troubles and beg Him to put them right... Those who are able to enclose themselves like this within the little heaven of their soul, wherein dwells the Creator of Heaven and earth, and have formed the habit of looking at nothing and staying in no place which will distract them, may be sure that they are walking on an excellent road and will without fail drink of the living water.

Way of Perfection c:28

DEALING WITH DISTRACTIONS

If you would go far on this road of prayer and ascend to the Mansion your heart is longing for, the important thing is not a lot of thinking but a lot of loving; so we must do whatever incites us to love.

Do not imagine that everything depends on never being distracted and that if you become a little distracted all is lost. Sometimes I myself have been troubled by mental turmoil and it is scarcely four years ago that I came to perceive clearly that only willed, deliberate thinking is a genuine distraction, not the thoughts or fancies that flow unbidden through our minds. Just as we cannot stop the revolving of the heavens, so we cannot stop the whirling of our fancies. We get worried and try to control them and consequently are diverted from our Lord, when perhaps our soul is united to God in a Mansion very near His own.

Interior Castle M:4 c:1

REAL PRAYER

The prayer that is most efficacious and
pleasing to God is the one that yields results.
I do not mean that, there and then, we should
feel fervent desires, for, although felt desires
are good, our self-love can easily overestimate
them. The best effects, in my opinion, are
those followed by actions, so that we do not
merely desire the honour of God but really
work for it, and use our minds thinking out
how best to please Him and show Him our
love more and more.

Even if at prayer I am pestered by severe
temptations and aridities and these make me
more humble, I count it good prayer, for what
I mean by the best prayer is that which pleases
God most. We must not think that because we
suffer in prayer we are not praying. Our very
sufferings are a prayer-offering and we may
well be praying much better than if we went
off into a corner and cracked our brains in
meditation.

Letter to Fr Jerome Gratian, 23 October 1576

HANDLE WITH CARE

Don't take any notice of the impulse to
give up in the middle of prayertime, just be
grateful for the desire to pray which is God's
gift. Your inmost heart loves to be with God
but feelings of sadness and depression weigh
you down and give you a sense of constraint.
When you feel like this, try to find a place
where you can see the sky and walk up and
down a little; that won't interfere with your
prayer in the least. We are human and have to
handle our frailty carefully so that we do not
overburden ourselves. Our hearts are seeking
God all the time, and we seek the means that
best lead us to Him. Our soul needs gentle
treatment.

Letter to Don Teutonio de Braganza, 3 July 1574

THE SACRED HUMANITY

In the beginning, when I had begun to make
a little progress in prayer… I thought I had a
sense of the presence of God… This sort of
prayer is often sweet and delightful. And so,
because I was conscious of the profit and
delight it afforded, no one could have brought
me back to contemplation of the Sacred
Humanity; for that seemed to me to be a real
hindrance to prayer… O Lord, what an evil
way I took! and I was straying from the way
if You had not brought me back to it. When
I see that You are near me, trials are easy to
bear… He helps, He strengthens, He never
fails, He is the true Friend. I see clearly, and
since then have always seen, that if we are
to please God and receive His great graces,
everything must pass through the hands of
His most Sacred Humanity… this is the door
by which we are to enter, if we would have His
supreme Majesty reveal to us His great secrets.

Life c:22

GOD AND THE SELF

THE ROAD TO HEAVEN

You must not be dismayed at the number of
things you have to consider before setting out
on this Divine journey which is the royal road
to Heaven. We gain such riches on this road
that it is no wonder that the cost seems high.
One day we shall realize that the price we have
paid is simply nothing at all compared with
the prize we have won. It is of the utmost
importance – I cannot stress this enough –
that those who wish to take this road in order
to drink of the water of life, must make a good
beginning by resolving with a most determined
determination never to stop until they reach
their goal; come what may, whatever happens
to them, however hard the labour, whoever may
complain of them, whether they reach their goal
or die on the road, or feel they no longer have
heart to face the trials they meet with; even if
the world should crumble under their feet.

Way of Perfection c:21

OUR GREATER GOOD

What can You do my Lord, that is not for the greater good of a soul that You know already belongs to You and which gives itself up to You, to follow You wherever You go, even to the death of the cross; one who is determined to help You carry that cross and not leave you alone with it? Such a one has nothing to fear. No, no, spiritual people have nothing to fear... Close the eyes of your imagination, and do not ask why God gives devotion to this person in so short a time, and none to me after so many years. We must believe that all is for our greater good; let His Majesty guide us whithersoever He will; we do not belong to ourselves but to God. It is privilege enough to be allowed to dig in God's garden and to be so near its owner. God is certainly near to us.

Life c:11

DOING GOD'S WILL

Wherein lies the highest perfection? Clearly,
not in interior consolations and raptures, nor
in visions or the spirit of prophecy, but in the
conforming of our will to the will of God, so
that there shall be nothing we know God wills
that we do not wholeheartedly will ourselves,
accepting the bitter as joyfully as the sweet
since we know it to be God's will. This seems
hard — not the mere doing of it, but the being
pleased in the doing of what is repugnant in
every way to our natural will. It is hard,
certainly, but love, if perfect, is strong enough
to do it and we forget our own pleasure in
order to please God who loves us so much…
our sufferings, no matter how great, become
sweet when we know that we are pleasing God.

Foundations c:5

SELF-OFFERING

Fix your eyes on the Crucified and nothing
else will be important to you. If His Majesty
showed His love for us by what He did,
expressing it in suffering beyond words, how
can you think to please Him with words alone?
Do you know what it is to be truly spiritual?
It is to become a slave of God, branded with
His seal, the sign of the Cross, a token that we
have handed ourselves over to Him. He is free
therefore, to sell us as slaves to the whole
world, just as He was, and be doing us no
wrong thereby, but rather a favour.

During the whole of this short life, which
may be much shorter for any of you than you
think, we must offer our Lord every possible
sacrifice, interior or exterior, and His Majesty
will unite our offering with the offering He
made of Himself to the Father on the Cross.

Interior Castle M:7 c:4

WALKING IN TRUTH

God can make us understand most vividly that He is absolute truth and cannot deceive. It is said in psalm 115, that every human being is a liar and by the light of this revelation we see the truth of this in a way we could never understand of ourselves, no matter how often we heard the words…

We must learn from this that if we are to become like our God who is our Spouse, we must apply ourselves most earnestly to walk in this truth. I am not meaning simply that we must not tell lies – that is taken for granted – I mean that we must walk in truth, in God's presence and before our fellow human beings to the very best of our ability and, in particular, we must not want to be thought better than we are and in all we do we must attribute to God what is rightly His and to ourselves what is ours, and seek the truth in everything.

Interior Castle M:6 c:10

THE HUMBLE HONEYBEE

How necessary self-knowledge is, even to those whom the Lord keeps with Himself in His own secret chamber! No matter how high a soul may have attained, self-knowledge is indispensable for it, and, in fact, the soul will not be able to escape awareness of its spiritual miseries, even if it should want to do so. Humility, like the honeybee busy making honey in the hive, must always be at work: without humility all is lost. Nevertheless, we have to remember that the bee also leaves the hive to fly foraging from flower to flower. Similarly, the soul must sometimes leave self-knowledge and soar aloft to consider the greatness and majesty of God. In so doing, it will come to a much better knowledge of its own lowliness than by always dwelling on itself.

Interior Castle M1 c:2

THE TEST OF TRUE LOVE

It is in the midst of temptation that love is
known, not in secret places; and believe me, our
gain will be incomparably greater, though there
may be more faults and even some tumbles…
We come to know what we are, and whether
our virtues are real. Someone always alone,
no matter how holy he imagines himself to be,
cannot possibly know whether he is patient
and humble and has no means of knowing.

O my God, if we only knew how wretched
we are!… I consider one day of humbling self-
knowledge, whatever the sorrow and distress
it has caused us, to be a greater grace of our
Lord than many days of prayer. However, a
true lover loves all the time and is always
remembering the beloved. It would be a sad
thing if we could pray only in secret places. I
see now that I cannot be alone for many hours.
But, O my Lord! how mighty before You is a
single sigh rising up from the heart…!

Foundations c:5

LOVE OF
NEIGHBOUR

THE TWO GREAT COMMANDMENTS

The Lord asks only two things of us: love for His Majesty and love for our neighbour. These are the two virtues we must strive for and if we keep these commandments perfectly, we are doing God's will and are united to Him. But how far we are from doing them in the way we ought for so great a God. The surest proof we have that we are really loving God is that we love our neighbour. We cannot be sure that we love God though there may be indications that we do, but we always know whether we are loving our neighbour or not. The greater our love for our neighbour, the greater is our love for God. His Majesty's love for each of us is so great, that He will reward the love we show to one another with a thousandfold increase of love for Him… I do not believe there can be great, selfless love for the neighbour that is not born of a deep love for God; our nature is too evil for that.

Interior Castle M:5 c:3

GENUINE LOVE

If only you grasped the importance of genuine
love for the neighbour, you would devote
yourselves completely to acquiring it. When
I see people anxious to know what stage of
prayer they have reached, so self-absorbed in
their prayer that they are afraid to stir or to
interrupt it with a thought lest they lose a jot
of the sweetness they are experiencing, I see
how little they understand of the road to
union. They imagine that this is what it is all
about. No, no; what our Lord looks for are the
works of love. If you have an opportunity of
helping a sick person, never fear that your
prayer will suffer; compassionate her; feel her
pain; go without food yourself rather than that
she should lack, and this, not so much for her
sake as because it is what our Lord asks of
you. This is union with our Lord's will. Again,
if you hear a person praised be more pleased
than if you were praised yourself; this is easy
enough if you are truly humble for then praise

would be painful. Be really glad when you see the goodness of other people and, equally, grieve to see them at fault, feeling for it as if it were you yourself, taking good care to conceal the fault from others.

Interior Castle M:5 c:3

FORGIVENESS IS ALL

Forgive us as we forgive. How much it means to
our Lord, this love of ours for one another! The
good Jesus might well have given precedence to
everything else rather than to love for one
another, and said: 'Forgive us, Lord, because
we do a lot of penance, we are often praying,
we have left everything for Your sake and we
love You very much'. He has never said:
'Because we would die for You'... He says
simply: 'Because we forgive'. I think the reason
for this is that He was well aware that our
wounded sensibilities and pride make mutual
love the hardest virtue to attain though it is
the one His Father values most... unless a
person is very determined and, when the
occasion arises makes a point of forgiving,
not just the mere nothings which people call
wrongs, but any wrong, no matter how great,
do not set store by that person's experiences
in prayer.

Way of Perfection c:36

OPEN YOUR MIND

A spiritual person, no matter how good,
will not attract others and lead them to
God if seen as narrow-minded and timorous.
These characteristics put people off, they feel
oppressed and frightened. And another thing
is that we may be critical of others, holier
than ourselves, because they do not act in
the same way as we do…

Try… to be as gracious as you can to
people without displeasing God in any way, so
that they enjoy talking to you and are drawn
to go your way and be like you, and not be
frightened by an austere face on virtue…
The holier people are, the more friendly they
should be with their associates, even though
they are not happy with their behaviour and
conversation. Do not keep aloof. You won't
help them that way. We must try hard to be
pleasant and get people to like us so that they
are drawn to love God. God, you know, is not
small-minded.

Way of Perfection c:41

UNION WITH GOD

GOD NEVER FAILS

I think I have received, as far as I can judge, a greater spiritual liberty. Hitherto, I thought I had need of others, and relied more on worldly helps. Now I clearly perceive that human beings are like bunches of dried rosemary, and that it is not safe to lean on them. If they are pressed down by things going wrong or malicious talk, they snap to pieces. And so I know now by experience that the only way not to fall is to cling to the cross and trust in Him who was nailed to it. He is my real Friend and, cleaving to Him, I find myself so strong that, so long as God never fails me, I think I could withstand the whole world if it were against me.

Relation 2

THE SPIRITUAL MARRIAGE

Oh, how far from wanting rest, how indifferent to praise, how devoid of desire for others' attention, will that person be in whom God has chosen to dwell in this special way! Completely occupied with Him, she will have no concern for herself. Her thoughts will be turned on how best to please Him and how to show Him more and more love. This is what prayer is all about; this is the purpose of the Spiritual Marriage of the soul with God; of it are born works that are pleasing to God. Good works are the unmistakable sign that God is working in the soul.

Interior Castle M:7 c:4

THE REWARDS OF LOVE

O Christians! for the love of the Lord, wake from sleep and remember that He does not keep us waiting until the next life before rewarding our love. He begins in this life.
O my Jesus! How I wish I could describe what we gain by throwing ourselves into our Lord's arms and entering into a covenant of love with Him whereby I devote myself utterly to the Beloved – 'I to my Beloved and my Beloved to me' – certain that, in His complete devotion to me, He can be trusted to take care of all my concerns and I will take care of His… Away from You I have no meaning. If I stray but a little from Your Majesty where shall I be?

O my Lord, Compassion itself and my sole Good! What more can I ask of life than to be so close to You that nothing whatever divides You and me. With Your companionship, what can prove too difficult? There is nothing I cannot undertake for Your love with Yourself so near.

Conceptions of the Love of God c:4

LOVE'S ARROW, LOVE'S SURRENDER

Love, I think, is an arrow shot by the will, and, freed from every pull of earth, flying straight at God with full force, it infallibly strikes His Majesty. Once it has pierced the Heart of God, absolute Love, it rebounds with immense graces...

O secrets of God! We must silence our understanding admitting that, never of itself can it fathom the greatness of God. Let us remember here Our Lady the Virgin, how she, in her great wisdom, surrendered in this way, and to her question to the angel, 'How shall this be done?', received the answer: 'The Holy Ghost will come upon you and the power of the Most High will overshadow you.'

Conceptions of the Love of God c:6

AT PEACE WITH GOD

Oh, what great happiness to be granted this
holy peace which compels the soul to wage war
on the whole world, whilst remaining at peace
in perfect security... It consists in being
united to God's will in such a way that there
is no distinction between God's will and the
soul's – they are one in reality, not merely in
words and desire. So ardent is the Bride's love
and in longing to please her Beloved, that
nothing can stop her once she understands
that by doing something she can serve Him
better... O strong love of God! I really do
believe that to one who loves, nothing seems
impossible. Happy the soul on whom God has
bestowed this peace. It has thereby become
sovereign over all the trials and dangers that
the world can offer...

Conceptions of the Love of God c:3

GOD IS ALL YOU NEED

Let nothing disturb you,
nothing make you afraid:
all things pass,
God remains.
Be patient,
and you will attain your heart's desire.
With God your own,
you cannot lack,
God suffices.

St Teresa's Bookmark

Text Acknowledgments

Extracts 1, 4, 5, 7, 10, 17, 18, 19, 21, 22 and 26 are taken from *Interior Castle*. Extracts 2 and 25 are taken from *Relations*. Extract 3 is taken from *Exclamations*. Extracts 6, 8, 9, 14, 23 and 24 are taken from *Way of Perfection*. Extracts 11 and 12 are taken from *Letters*. Extracts 13 and 15 are taken from *Life*. Extracts 16 and 20 are taken from *Foundations*. Extracts 27, 28 and 29 are taken from *Conceptions of the Love of God*. Extract 30 is taken from *St Teresa's Bookmark*.

Picture Acknowledgments

Illustrations on pages 1, 2, 6, 16 and 47 are reproduced courtesy of Bridgeman Art Library. Page 1: *The Annunciation* (panel), by Spanish School, 1581, Museo de Santa Cruz, Toledo, Spain. Page 2: *Christ Resurrected between St Theresa of Avila and St John of the Cross*, by Michel des Gobelins Corneille (1642–1708), Chapelle Saint-Joseph des Carmes, Paris, France. Page 6: *Meeting between St John of the Cross and St Theresa of Avila*, by French School (16th century), Bibliotheque Nationale, Paris, France. Page 16: *The Annunciation* (panel), by Juan de Borgona (1495–1533), Museo de Santa Cruz, Toledo, Spain. Page 47 and cover: *St Theresa of Avila*, by Juan de la Miseria (c.1526–1616), Convent of St Theresa, Avila, Spain.

Illustrations on pages 11 and 35 are reproduced courtesy of The National Gallery, London. Page 11: *The Two Trinities*, by Bartolomé Esteban Murillo. Page 35: *Christ Healing the Paralytic at the Pool of Bethesda*, by Bartolomé Esteban Murillo.

Illustrations on pages 19, 27 and 41 are reproduced courtesy of SuperStock Ltd. Page 19: *Temptation of Christ in the Wilderness*, by Juan de Flandes. Page 27: *The Crucified Christ*, by Francisco de Zurbaran. Page 41: *Christ the Host*, by Juan Vincente Macip.